*Nothing has changed
but my attitude.
Everything has changed.*

Anthony de Mello

Other Health Communications Books by Bryan E. Robinson

Work Addiction:
Hidden Legacies Of Adult Children.

Soothing Moments:
Daily Meditations For Fast Track Living.

Heal Your Self-Esteem:
Recovery From Addictive Thinking.

Stressed Out?
A Guidebook For Taking Care Of Yourself.

Healograms 1: How To Take Care Of Yourself

Healograms 3: How To Resolve The Conflict In Your Life

Healograms 4: How To Make Your Life A Miracle

HEALOGRAMS
2
HOW TO LIVE YOUR LIFE TO THE FULLEST

Bryan E. Robinson, Ph.D.

Health Communications, Inc.
Deerfield Beach, Florida

Bryan E. Robinson, Ph.D.
University of North Carolina at Charlotte
Charlotte, North Carolina

©1991 Bryan E. Robinson
ISBN 1-55874-188-7

All rights reserved. Printed in the United States of America. No part of this publication may be reproduced, stored in a retrieval system or transmitted in any form or by any means, electronic, mechanical, photocopying, recording or otherwise without the written permission of the publisher.

Publisher: Health Communications, Inc.
3201 S.W. 15th Street
Deerfield Beach, Florida 33442-8190

Cover design by Graphic Expressions

INTRODUCTION
How Healograms Work

Healograms are positive, healthy messages we send to ourselves. They help us combat the old negative messages we got when growing up — the harmful thoughts that still blink in our brain like a neon sign. They help us unravel ourselves from addictive relationships so that we can feel our own feelings, make our own decisions, be our own person and stand on our own two feet. They help us to achieve a higher quality of life and live it more fully.

This booklet contains written *Healograms* on a variety of topics that can help you recover from co-dependency. Reflect on each of the messages and silently apply them to your own life. Then become actively involved in the healing process as you write your own *Healograms* with four key questions to guide you:

1. What has kept you from affirming the healthy message in the past?
2. Why is it important for you to affirm the message?
3. What steps will you take to affirm the message in your personal life?
4. When will you take this action?

If you are a people pleaser, if you are driven by "shoulds," "oughts" and other shame-based messages, if you put everyone else's needs before your own, if you are living your life for everyone but yourself, *Healograms* can help you take positive steps for a more fulfilling life. These affirming messages give direction to your life by guiding you through each day and reminding you to live with hope and optimism. They show you how to empower yourself and how to restore meaning, quality and balance to your life.

SAMPLE

Healograms
Speaking Up For Myself

What has kept me from doing it?
I have always let my spouse speak for me.
I always thought that if I spoke up,
people wouldn't listen because my ideas
don't really matter much.

Why is it important for me to do it?
So that I can feel as if I count for something
instead of feeling like a second-rate person.

What will I do to make it happen?

When we go to a restaurant, my spouse always orders for me whatever he wants, so we both end up eating the same thing. From now on, I plan to order what I want for myself. Next time, I will also help choose the restaurant, which I never do. I will start speaking up about my likes and dislikes in all other areas of my life too.

When will I do it?

The next time my spouse and I eat out at a restaurant, which is usually every Friday night. Also at work when I eat lunch with co-workers, I will start making suggestions about where I want to eat.

HEALOGRAMS

How To Live Our Lives To The Fullest

1. Feeling Our Own Feelings 1
2. Living Our Lives In The Present ... 5
3. Permitting Ourselves
   To Make Mistakes 9
4. Holding To Our Convictions 13
5. Releasing Our Resentments 17
6. Owning Ourselves And
   Dispossessing Others 21
7. Taking Healing Action
   In Our Lives 25
8. Exercising Our Choices 29
9. Lifting Our Sagging Spirits 33
10. Evaluating Our Relationships 37

11.	Finding The Blessings In Our Hardships	41
12.	Severing Our Unhealthy Ties	45
13.	Expressing Our Gratitude	49
14.	Being Patient With Ourselves	53
15.	Connecting With The Joy In Our Lives	57

Feeling Our Own Feelings

There may be a part of us that doesn't like disappointing others. We may be afraid of making someone angry. When we are obsessed with the effect our actions will have on others, we are never able to live our lives to suit ourselves.

We decide what mood we're in *after* we get to work so that it matches the emotions of our boss. We wait until we get home to gauge how we feel by the emotions of our loved ones. When others are tense, we become tense. When others are happy, we allow ourselves to be happy.

In recovery from co-dependency we learn that if someone gets mad or disappointed, that's not our fault. We accept responsibility for *our* feelings but not for the feelings and actions of others. We make decisions about our thoughts and feelings regardless of the moods of loved ones and friends. As we heal, we understand that the only way to achieve true happiness is to live our lives by *our* own inner values and by developing *our* own standards of acceptance. We are not bent and swayed by what other people think but feel comfortable with our own inner sense of who we are.

*We accept responsibility for **our** feelings but not for the feelings and actions of others.*

Living Our Lives In The Present

We live in the future or dwell in the past. We often find it difficult to pay attention to the present moment. We don't really see the people we are with. We miss the beauty of a sunset, a child's small trusting hand, a bouquet of red roses. We miss long walks and heart-to-heart talks with friends and loved ones. As long as we skip the present, we have no life because the past is already gone and the future never arrives. All we have is the moment.

Carpe diem, Latin for "seize the day," reminds us to live in the now because the present is the most valuable time we ever have. It advises us to live our lives fully, not fretting about what went wrong or worrying about what will happen.

We can begin living for today and resist our mind's attempts to preoccupy us with yesterday, tomorrow or next week. From this moment we can start anew. We only have the now and we can live it to the fullest.

Today is the day to tell someone we love them, make a confession or mend a relationship. This is the day to appreciate our lives and live fully in the moment.

Today is the day to tell someone we love them, make a confession or mend a relationship. This is the day to appreciate our lives and live fully in the moment.

_____

_____

_____

_____

_____

_____

_____

_____

_____

_____

Permitting Ourselves To Make Mistakes

Sometimes when we make mistakes, we feel that *we* are the mistakes. If we do something wrong, shame and guilt surface as we confuse the action with ourselves and jam them all together in our minds. We feel that we are bad human beings.

We are compelled to *prove* ourselves, rather than just *be* ourselves. Being ourselves means being wrong sometimes and right sometimes.

When we make a mistake, that doesn't mean we *are* the mistake. We expect and permit ourselves to make mistakes and stop berating ourselves when we do. We give up our alibis for our shortcomings by admitting them without self-condemnation.

Everyone falls short at one time or another and failure is a natural part of being human. Once we accept our human imperfections, we get rid of our fear of disappointing others or making someone angry. We release our negative self-doubts and allow ourselves to be human. When we make mistakes, we admit our wrongdoing without shame and guilt and continue to love and care for ourselves. Self-forgiveness becomes part of our human condition.

When we make mistakes, we admit our wrongdoing without shame and guilt and continue to love and care for ourselves.

4

Holding To Our Convictions

A colleague makes an unreasonable request and we say no. We put limits on a friend's habit of taking advantage. We refuse to bail out a loved one from a predicament he keeps repeating.

We feel a tinge of guilt but we hold to our convictions. The colleague may tell us we're inconsiderate. The friend may say we're selfish. The loved one may say we're unloving. But for the first time in our lives we have drawn the line. Convictions triumph over guilt.

We have broken through the bounds of co-dependency by taking care of ourselves instead of meeting the needs of others at our own expense. We don't allow others to manipulate us with this disfavor. We can live with ourselves because we do what we believe to be right and we know we are doing what's best. Old feelings of guilt, failure and self-hatred are replaced with feelings of self-respect and self-love.

We can live with ourselves because we do what we believe to be right and we know we are doing what's best.

Releasing Our Resentments

Holding resentments against those who hurt, embarrass or reject us blocks our healing path. We can ask ourselves what purpose hanging on to these feelings serves. Perhaps it is one way of retaliation, our way of punishing the ones who harmed us. Maybe we harbor old hurts because we feel sorry for ourselves.

Sometimes we get addicted to holding on to grudges because we get emotional satisfaction from them. We think we need them. We don't want to let go. We may even be afraid that if we let them go, there will be nothing left of us. Carrying a chip on our shoulder only hurts ourselves. It weighs us down, eats away at us and keeps us stuck in misery and defeat.

Forgiving others for the wrongs they commit is the ultimate act of self-love because it rids us of hurt and frees us of emotional and physical harm. Acts of forgiveness are done for our benefit, not for someone else's. We can set ourselves free by forgiving the wrongdoer and ourselves and releasing resentments one by one.

Forgiving others for the wrongs they commit is the ultimate act of self-love because it rids us of hurt and frees us of emotional and physical harm.

_____
_____
_____
_____
_____
_____
_____
_____
_____
_____
_____

6

Owning Ourselves And Dispossessing Others

We possess things; we love people. Too few of us follow this. How many of us, in fact, follow the reverse? We possess people; we love things. Healing from co-dependency teaches us that we don't own people and we can never possess them. Ownership gives us a feeling of power and control, the need for which comes from our own deep insecurities.

In truth, the only possessions we have are ourselves. Recovery helps us to own our thoughts, feelings and behaviors and to treat others as separate human beings, not as objects of ownership.

We do not need possessions to make us complete. Possessing another person or thing does not satisfy an inner need. Attaining inner harmony extinguishes the need to possess things or people. Serenity from knowing that we are complete reduces our need to own anyone or anything.

Serenity from knowing that we are complete reduces our need to own anyone or anything.

7

Taking Healing Action In Our Lives

Healing comes from action, not lethargy. Nothing ventured, nothing gained. Setting boundaries, taking risks, making choices, going with the fear, being optimistic — are all healing actions. We can risk being called silly, being contradicted or being criticized but the risk makes us stronger.

We can dare to heal ourselves by taking a new course of action — by standing up and going forward, rather than plopping down and going backwards. We stand up and speak out in our best interests. We can take a new approach to solving old problems and stop using old ways that don't work. We can stop going back to the same people for the same rejections. If something's not working, we can do something about it. If that doesn't work, we can do something else. When we persist with another course of action, we eventually solve our problems.

We can dare to heal ourselves by taking a new course of action — by standing up and going forward, rather than plopping down and going backwards.

Exercising Our Choices

Choice. It's one of our greatest resources and all of us have it available. It's up to each and every one of us to create the kind of life that we want. The one thing no one can take away from us is the power of choice. No matter how horrendous our yesterdays, we can choose to transform them into happy and fulfilling todays and tomorrows.

No matter how difficult things seem, we *always* have choices. People and situations do not make decisions for us unless we allow them to. We have more choices than we ever realized and we can increase our options in favor of a happy and fulfilling life.

We open ourselves to new experiences and transform our old realities. We can choose one thing to do differently, no matter how small, that we have never done before. We can take a different route home from work, do something different in our lunch hours, start a new hobby, take a new challenge that used to frighten us. Then we can stand back and watch ourselves grow from the new experience.

No matter how horrendous our yesterdays, we can choose to transform them into happy and fulfilling todays and tomorrows.

Lifting Our Sagging Spirits

Sometimes we reach the lowest point in our healing process. Our spirit sags, we are blue — full of anxiety, frustration and irritability. Being lonely, sad and tense are normal human feelings that everyone has from time to time. These are the tough times that accompany recovery from co-dependency. Sometimes we have to take three steps backward before leaping ten steps forward but falling back is part of moving forward.

Just when we feel we can fall no lower and our situation is hopeless, a miracle happens. We fall up, not down. We fall into light, not darkness, and see the way out of our predicament.

Belief in a Higher Power restores us with hope when we are down. When all else is gone, our Higher Power is always there to guide us through the mist and into the light. On days when we feel like giving up, we can remember that these days are part of the recovery process. Accepting the lows with the highs gives us hope for tomorrow and strength to endure today. Knowing that this too shall pass gives a new lift for our sagging spirits.

Sometimes we have to take three steps backward before leaping ten steps forward but falling back is part of moving forward.

_____
_____
_____
_____
_____
_____
_____
_____
_____
_____
_____
_____

Evaluating Our Relationships

Do we continue to get involved in relationships with people who emotionally reject us? Do we make ourselves a doormat for others so that they will love and approve of us? Or do we surround ourselves with people who affirm our beauty and worth?

We unconsciously surround ourselves with people with whom we feel comfortable and familiar. When we are troubled and confused, we are attracted to troubled and disturbed personalities. The company we keep rubs off on us and we on them. We influence each other's thoughts and behaviors through a cycle of interactions.

Breaking our attraction to unhealthy relationships begins with our own self-acceptance and self-love. We break this cycle by taking stock of the company we keep. We avoid those who put us down and detract from our personal healing, and we keep the company of affirming people. We seek out relationships with people who affirm our true value and who help us grow and fulfill our potential. We find ourselves surrounded with people who love and care for themselves and who mirror our own inner beauty and self-worth.

We seek out relationships with people who affirm our true value and who help us grow and fulfill our potential.

Finding The Blessings In Our Hardships

Life is full of ups and downs. Understanding and dealing with this fundamental truth is part of recovery. We can strap ourselves in for the ride and after the bumps we can get up again — better than ever.

There are good times and bad times, highs and lows, joys and sadness. We get hired and fired. We get recognized and overlooked, we get loved and rejected and we get credit and blame. Sometimes we feel great and other times small.

Blessings often come to us in disguise. Knowing we cannot change the ups and downs of life but can only adjust our inner selves helps us put pain, loss and hardship into their proper perspective. We can always find good in the bad when we look for it. We begin to see more beauty than flaws, more hope than despair. We see blessings and constructive outcomes even in loss and disappointment.

We see blessings and constructive outcomes even in loss and disappointment.

Severing Our Unhealthy Ties

Staying in unhealthy relationships is damaging to us because it sends the message that we are not worthy of better. As we start to get healthier, our relationships automatically undergo change. We find it almost impossible to stay in relationships with others who continue their addictive ways. We see the unhealthy patterns more clearly and are repelled rather than attracted. The old ways no longer feel comfortable. It's like trying to wear old clothes that no longer fit.

As we recover from co-dependency, some long-time friendships fall by the wayside along with many of our old habits. But we find new, healthier friendships to replace the old ones. Sometimes it's sad to let go of old friends but it may be necessary. Our friendships are a reflection of who we are inside. When we begin to heal, we are different from the old self. Healthier relationships are part of a trade for a healthier way of being.

We do not let old relationships hold us back from our personal growth. We value relationships, new and old, that reflect the new us.

We do not let old relationships hold us back from our personal growth.

Expressing Our Gratitude

If diamonds lay in piles beside the interstate highway, we wouldn't even take the time to stop for one. But if there was one diamond in the world, it would be priceless. We want what we cannot have and we devalue what we do have simply because we have it. When we define our happiness in terms of what is missing from our lives, we operate from a point of lack and discontent. We fool ourselves into thinking that something or someone will fill that void and make us complete.

We gripe and complain about minor inconveniences when our lives are already rich and full. Sometimes it takes a jolt for us to realize how truly fortunate we are. The day-to-day annoyances we complain about are suddenly trivial when we face a major catastrophe. We can count our blessings, be thankful for all that we have and save complaining for the rare and important obstacles in life. Happiness comes from wanting what we already have and expressing gratitude for it.

Happiness comes from wanting what we already have and expressing gratitude for it.

_____
_____
_____
_____
_____
_____
_____
_____
_____
_____
_____
_____

Being Patient With Ourselves

Having lived our lives in co-dependent relationships for so long, we must be patient as we begin our recovery. We cannot expect to change old thoughts and behaviors in one day, week or even a month. It has taken us years to get into our present fix and it will take time to undo the negative patterns. Impatience in recovery sabotages our spiritual growth.

Recovery from co-dependency is a process in which we are always getting better and better and the quality of our lives is always improving. We can feel ourselves getting healthier and happier, day by day.

When our personal growth does not seem to be moving fast enough, we need not become discouraged. Reminding ourselves that important things take time helps us to be patient with the process. We are on our Higher Power's schedule, not our own. Our healing is already working when we admit we are powerless over the ability to control our lives. Patience helps us slow down and lets the process work the way it is supposed to.

Patience helps us slow down and lets the process work the way it is supposed to.

Connecting With
The Joy In Our Lives

Sometimes we take life's challenges so seriously, we think our healing from co-dependency has to be all work and no play. We get so used to moping and crying about our problems, we forget there is a flip side to life. We become so accustomed to grabbing onto others' pain and hurt that we miss riding our own wave of joy. Life is not 100% serious business. Joy and light-hearted fun help us heal too. Looking at our situations from a different slant can lift the cloud of despair that sometimes hangs over our heads.

We don't wait for someone else to be joyful before we allow ourselves to express it. We don't have to have a reason to be joyful. We can simply choose it, regardless of the moods of those around us. Joy is all around us and within us. All we have to do is connect with it. No matter what happens at the office or at home, we can look at the lighter side of life, try not to take ourselves too seriously and balance our days with joy and laughter whenever we can.

...y is all around us and within us. All we ...ve to do is connect with it.